Chameleons

By Erika and Jim Deiters

ANIMALS OF THE RAINFOREST

www.raintreepublishers.co.uk

Visit our website to find out more information about Raintree books.

To order:
☎ Phone 44 (0) 1865 888112
▤ Send a fax to 44 (0) 1865 314091
🖳 Visit the Raintree Bookshop at www.raintreepublishers.co.uk to browse our catalogue and order online.

First published in Great Britain by Raintree Publishers, Halley Court, Jordan Hill, Oxford, OX2 8EJ, part of Harcourt Education.
Raintree is a registered trademark of Harcourt Education Ltd.

Originated by Dot Gradations Ltd
Printed and bound in Hong Kong and China by South China

ISBN 1 844 21102 9
07 06 05 04 03
10 9 8 7 6 5 4 3 2 1

British Library Cataloguing in Publication Data
Deiters, Erika
Chameleons - (Animals of the rainforest)
1. Chameleons - Juvenile literature
2. Rain forest ecology - Juvenile literature
I.Title II.Deiters, Jim
597.9'5
A catalogue for this book is available from the British Library.

Acknowledgements
Photophile/Robert Metzgus, p. **11**
Visuals Unlimited/Jim Merli, pp. **1, 22**; Tom J. Ulrich, pp. **6, 12**; Don W. Fawcett, p. **14**; Joe McDonald, pp. **5, 16, 19, 20, 24, 26, 27**; Wildlife Conservation Society, p. **8**.

Cover photograph by Tom J. Ulrich.

Every effort has been made to contact copyright holders of any material reproduced in this book. Any omissions will be rectified in subsequent printings if notice is given to the publishers.

Contents

Any words appearing in the text in bold, **like this**, are explained in the Glossary.

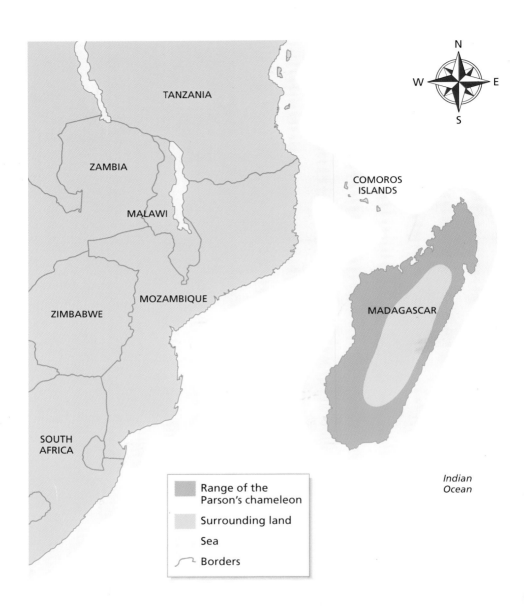

	Range of the Parson's chameleon
	Surrounding land
	Sea
	Borders

TANZANIA

ZAMBIA

MALAWI

ZIMBABWE

MOZAMBIQUE

SOUTH AFRICA

COMOROS ISLANDS

MADAGASCAR

Indian Ocean

A quick look at chameleons

What do chameleons look like?
Chameleons have long, flattened bodies. Their backs are high and rounded. They have large heads, and their eyes bulge. They are usually brown, green or grey, and can change their colours in only a few seconds.

Where do chameleons live?
Most chameleons live in the rainforests of Africa and Madagascar. Madagascar is an island off the south-east coast of Africa. A few kinds of chameleons live in southern Europe and Asia.

What do chameleons eat?
Chameleons eat all kinds of insects, including grasshoppers, moths, dragonflies, caterpillars and crickets. They lick dewdrops and raindrops from leaves when they are thirsty.

Chameleons live in rainforest trees.

Chameleons in the rainforest

Chameleons have been around since the time of the dinosaurs. The scientific name for the chameleon family is *Chamaeleontidae*.

Chameleons live almost everywhere in Africa and Madagascar. Most live in the rainforest. Rainforests are warm places where many trees and plants grow close together and a lot of rain falls. Chameleons can also live in the dry sands of the desert or high in the mountains. A few **species** live in southern Europe and Asia. A species is a group of animals or plants most closely related to each other.

Many trees and plants in the rainforest provide food and shelter for chameleons.

The Parson's chameleon is the largest species of chameleon.

Cold-blooded reptiles

Chameleons are **reptiles**. A reptile is a **cold-blooded** animal. The body of a cold-blooded animal warms or cools to about the same temperature as the air or water around it.

Chameleons are lizards. Yet they are unlike other lizards. They cannot grow new tails. If other lizards lose their tails, most can grow a new one. Chameleons also move more slowly than other lizards.

Kinds of rainforest chameleon

There are about 100 kinds of chameleon. About half live on the island of Madagascar. The Parson's chameleon is the largest chameleon. It can grow to almost 91 centimetres long. Other chameleons on the island are so small that spiders eat them.

The group of chameleons called stump-tailed chameleons are the smallest chameleons. They grow to less than 2.5 centimetres long. They are grey and brown. Their colour helps them blend in with the rainforest floor where they live. Their feet are covered with small **scales**. Scales are overlapping pieces of hard skin. These help the chameleons grip the ground.

The Namaqua chameleon lives in Africa. It is also called the leaf chameleon. It looks like a dead leaf. It is usually brown and has a short tail. It spends most of the time on the ground and is not as colourful as most chameleons.

Appearance

Chameleons have large heads. Their eyes bulge and are almost completely covered with skin. They can move each of their eyes in a different direction. One eye can look forwards while the other looks backwards.

Chameleons have long, flattened bodies. Their backs are high and rounded. Their shape helps them balance on branches. Their shoulder blades move with their legs. This helps them reach further out.

Chameleons have five toes on each of their feet. Their front feet have three toes on the inside and two toes on the outside. The toes on their back feet are the opposite, with two toes inside and three outside. This lets the chameleons grip things well. They also have sharp claws.

Chameleon have prehensile tails that can be longer than their bodies. They can wrap their tails around branches and hang from trees. They can also use their tails to grip branches as they climb. They roll up their tails to rest.

Male and female chameleons look different from each other. Males have thicker tails. They are also more colourful than females.

▲ This chameleon has three horns on its head.

Some kinds of chameleon have horns. They may have from one to four horns. Some have crests on top of their heads. A crest is a natural growth on the head of an animal.

All chameleons are covered with scales. These are made of a material called keratin. People's fingernails are also made of keratin.

▲ **This chameleon's green colour helps it blend in with plant and tree leaves.**

Colouring

Chameleons are usually brown, green or grey. Their normal colour helps them blend in with their background. Colours, shapes and patterns that help animals hide are called **camouflage**.

Sunlight, temperature and mood make some chameleons change their colour. They do not change colour to hide, as many people believe. When it is cold, their skin turns darker. Darker colours help them soak up the warm sunlight.

Chameleons turn brown if they are cold, sleepy or sick. They turn yellow when they give up in a fight. When they are angry, they show bright colours. If they are very angry, they turn black.

How chameleons live

Most chameleons are **arboreal**. This means they live in trees. In a rainforest, the area of thick leaves and branches above the ground is called the **canopy**. The canopy provides a place to hide from **predators**. Predators are animals that hunt other animals and eat them. Chameleons sit still and use their normal colouring as camouflage to hide from predators.

Chameleons are not social. They like to live alone. They make their homes in different parts of the canopy. The canopy has lower, middle and upper parts. Some chameleons like to live in the upper canopy, about 45 metres above the ground. The lower and middle canopy are from 6 metres to 30 metres above the ground. Some chameleons live there. Others live on the ground.

This chameleon has puffed itself up to look larger while it defends its territory.

A chameleon's day

Chameleons are active during the day. The warmth of the sun gives them energy. Their skin holds the heat. Chameleons must be careful not to overheat. They cool off in the shade of the trees.

Chameleons rock back and forth when they move through the branches. This makes them look like leaves blowing in the wind. Moving in this way helps them hide from predators. It also allows them to sneak up on prey. Prey are the animals that predators hunt and eat.

Chameleons are **territorial**. A territorial animal lives on, and fights to keep, an area for itself. Chameleons defend their homes in the trees. They try to scare off other chameleons. They hiss, puff up their bodies or show their teeth. They fight only if this show does not work.

Chameleons usually return to the same sleeping spot each night. They often sleep at the tip of a branch. This prevents a heavy predator, such as a leopard, from coming too close. A chameleon will even drop from a branch if it feels a predator's movement. It is able to quickly fill its body with air. This helps soften the fall. The puffed-up body floats if it lands in water.

This chameleon is hunting. Its tongue
is curled in its mouth, ready to strike.

What chameleons eat

Chameleons are carnivores. Carnivores are animals that eat only other animals. Chameleons eat all kinds of insect, including grasshoppers, moths and caterpillars. The trees where chameleons live are good hunting grounds.

Animals that eat insects must be careful. Some insects protect themselves with stings and poison. The bearded chameleon, however, eats bees and does not get hurt. The Pardalis chameleon is able to eat spiders that make other animals ill.

Larger chameleons sometimes eat smaller lizards or other animals. The Meller's chameleon eats young birds. It takes them from their nests.

Chameleons lick dewdrops and raindrops from the leaves when they are thirsty.

How chameleons catch food

To catch food, chameleons climb to a spot in the branches. They blend in with the rainforest treetops. Their prey cannot see them.

Chameleons sit and wait for their prey to come to them. Some place themselves among flowering trees and bushes. The flowers attract insects.

Chameleons have a poor sense of smell and hearing. But they can see very well. Chameleons can move their eyes separately in all directions to look for their prey. When the prey is close, chameleons point both eyes towards it.

Chameleons have long tongues. They pack their tongues in the back of their mouths. When they see prey, chameleons bring their tongues to the front of their mouths. They have a special tongue bone. It helps them aim their tongues at their prey. Their tongues are rough and covered with sticky saliva. Prey stick to them.

Chameleons have two sets of muscles in their tongue. One muscle allows it to grab prey. The other muscle helps them pull their tongue back in. They can shoot their tongue out and pull it back in sixteen times per second.

▲ **This chameleon is eating an insect.**

Chameleons have teeth on the rims of their jaws. They use their teeth to grind their food. A chameleon sits in the sun after it eats. The warmth of the sun helps it **digest** its food. The bodies of cold-blooded animals digest food faster when they are warmer.

A chameleon can die if it becomes too cold after eating. The prey will rot in its stomach and poison the chameleon.

When a chameleon grows, it will shed its old skin so new skin can replace it.

A chameleon's life cycle

Male chameleons become very colourful during the mating season. They use bright colours to attract females. Sometimes females will change colour to show that they are not interested in the males.

Males also fight over females. These fights usually do not involve physical contact. Males puff up and hiss at other males to try to scare them away. The losing male turns darker green and walks away.

A male's face becomes red when he is ready to mate. The rims of his lips become yellow. The yellow lips are a sign to other males to keep away. The yellow is also a sign to females that the male is ready to mate. If a female is coloured black with orange patterns, she is carrying young.

▲ **This female is digging a hole to bury her eggs.**

Eggs

Most chameleons lay eggs. The mother lays up to 50 eggs. She buries the eggs in the ground. Female chameleons leave after laying their eggs. The eggs remain buried for several months. They have many tiny holes that allow air and water to enter. The young chameleons breathe and drink while they are in the egg. They can die in the egg if the ground is too hot. They can also drown if the ground is too wet.

Young chameleons are able to stop growing inside the egg. This ability is called **diapause**. It allows them to wait for the right conditions before hatching. The ground has to be soft enough for them to crawl out of the buried nest. Once out, the young have to survive on their own.

Young chameleons

Chameleons never stop growing. They shed their skins as their bodies grow larger, just like snakes. They grow the most and shed the most during their first year.

Young chameleons are in great danger. Many animals of the rainforest prey on them. Young chameleons are usually grey or brown. These colours camouflage them against the trees. They can change colour and puff themselves up. This makes them look larger. If they look larger, some animals may be afraid of them.

Nobody knows how long chameleons can live in the wild. Scientists think they live for about two years. They have survived for up to ten years in captivity.

Without their rainforest habitat, chameleons would die out.

The future of chameleons

Like many wild animals, chameleons are losing their **habitat**. The rainforests of Africa and Madagascar are disappearing. People are cutting down trees to make room for new homes and farms. They are also selling the wood from trees. Chameleons cannot survive without the forests.

Traders buy chameleons and sell them as pets. Chameleons, however, do not make good pets. When taken from the wild, chameleons usually die within a few weeks. That is because they need a certain amount of sun and certain temperatures to live. It is hard for people to create the conditions chameleons need to live.

This chameleon has wrapped its tail around a branch.

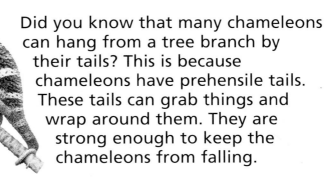

Did you know that many chameleons can hang from a tree branch by their tails? This is because chameleons have prehensile tails. These tails can grab things and wrap around them. They are strong enough to keep the chameleons from falling.

What will happen to chameleons?

Some scientists are trying to breed chameleons to release in the wild. They are having a hard time. Only a few chameleons have been born.

Many people understand that chameleons are important to life in the rainforests. In some places, it is now against the law to remove them from the rainforests or sell them. Without laws, the sale and removal of chameleons from their habitats would probably increase.

Laws are not enough. People must make sure that the laws are obeyed. They must report people who break the laws. They must teach other people about the importance of chameleons. Laws and learning may help people keep chameleons alive in their rainforest homes for a very long time.

head
see page 10

eyes
see pages 10, 18

scales
see pages 9, 11

toes
see page 10

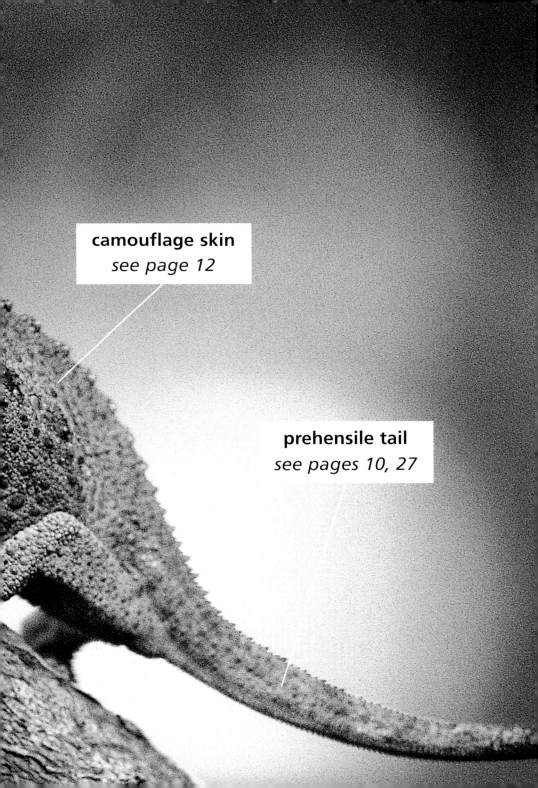

camouflage skin
see page 12

prehensile tail
see pages 10, 27

Glossary

arboreal living mainly in trees

camouflage colours, shapes and patterns that make something blend in with its background

canopy (KAN-uh-pee) thick area of leaves high up in the treetops

cold-blooded animals with body temperatures that change according to their surroundings

diapause animal's ability to control its development within an egg

digest to break down food for the body to use

habitat place where an animal or plant usually lives

predator animal that hunts other animals to eat

reptile cold-blooded animal with a tough skin covered in scales

scales small overlapping pieces of thick, hard skin that cover an animal's body

species a group of animals or plants most closely related to each other

territorial animal that defends the land it has claimed as its home

Internet sites

Enchanted Learning
www.EnchantedLearning.com/subjects/rainforest

Rainforest Education
www.animalsoftherainforest.org

Useful address

World Wildlife Fund-UK
Panda House, Weyside Park
Godalming, Surrey, GU7 1XR

Books to read

Theodorou, R; Telford, C. *Amazing Journeys: Up
a Rainforest Tree. Heinemann Library, Oxford,
1998*

Index